Petite Eats

Appetizers, Tasters, Miniature Desserts, and More

Petite Eats

Appetizers, Tasters, Miniature Desserts, and More

TIMOTHY W. LAWRENCE

Skyhorse Publishing

Skyhorse Publishing books may be purchased in bulk at special discounts for sales promotion, corporate gifts, fund-raising, or educational purposes. Special editions can also be created to specifications. For details, contact the Special Sales Department, Skyhorse Publishing, 307 West 36th Street, 11th Floor, New York, NY 10018 or info@skyhorsepublishing.com.

Skyhorse® and Skyhorse Publishing® are registered trademarks of Skyhorse Publishing, Inc.®, a Delaware corporation.

Visit our website at www.skyhorsepublishing.com.

10 9 8 7 6 5 4 3 2 1

Library of Congress Cataloging-in-Publication Data is available on file.

ISBN: 978-1-62087-400-4

Printed in China

{ Contents }

{ Introduction }

W hen I first heard about a "tasting" party, my mind immediately went to wine, cheese, and chocolate. But as tasting parties rise in popularity, the menus are also expanding. Similar to *tapas* in Spanish cuisine, tasting parties are an opportunity for a host to showcase a wide variety of culinary creations in smaller portions. Almost any dish—very basic to very elegant—can be scaled down and served as a taster. The purpose of this book is to show how, with a little basic knowledge and a few simple skills, anyone can host a great tasting party with their favorite foods!

I've loved cooking for as long as I can remember, largely due to the fact that my mom is a great cook. Fresh, local, real ingredients: These are the keys to great cooking, whether you're preparing large or small portions, cooking entire meals or simple snacks. The fresher your ingredients, the less skill, time, and cost are required to produce something delicious. Think about it: What's simpler and more satisfying to the palate than a tomato picked straight from the garden, sliced, and served with a few basil leaves?

Not everyone has direct access to a garden for fresh produce or a farm for fresh meat or dairy products, and so it is perfectly acceptable to use the freshest ingredients your budget and local grocery store or farmer's market can provide. But there are a few ingredients that should never be substituted. Maple syrup, for example, should never be replaced with commercial maple-flavored syrups in these recipes. The results will be very disappointing. In the same vein, butter should never be replaced with margarine, and real vanilla extract will always yield noticeably better results than imitation vanilla extract. Other than that, don't stress too much about substituting ingredients to fit your tastes or resources.

The recipes here exhibit a mix of different foods and preparations with the hope of inspiring you to host your own tasting party. But don't stop with what's in this book—once you've explored these recipes, you should have a better sense of how any of your favorite dishes can be presented creatively in miniature form.

While putting this book together, I was reminded that sometimes the most satisfying dishes are also the simplest. I've always believed that anyone with a little knowledge can prepare delicious, stunning food without needing fancy, expensive ingredients or cookware.

I would like to thank my parents for their continuing support and love for me, and my mom for her love of cooking.

I too would like to thank my wife, Abbey, for all of her love and support through the years—you've helped me more than you will ever know.

Thanks also to the Lord God for His inspiration and opportunities in this venture!

And finally, you, the reader of this book! I hope you find it inspiring.

{ Tasting Party Tips }

When planning a tasting party, consider making it themed. Here are a few ideas:

- Seasonal Tasting: Feature a food or several foods that are at their seasonal peak. For example, a spring menu might include prosciutto-wrapped asparagus (page 33), artichoke dip in a bread bowl (page 68), bacon-wrapped dates with maple sauce (page 15), and chocolate covered strawberries (page 86).
- Dessert Tasting: Serve only desserts and accompany with a selection of coffees, teas, and homemade hot chocolate (page 122).
- International Tasting: For example, a Mexican tasting might include taco cups (page 67), salsa and guacamole with chips (page 66), black bean dip, and margaritas.

When planning your menu, choose five to seven different dishes. If you do more than that, you're likely to end up spending the whole party in the kitchen. A big point of hosting a tasting party is to enjoy the time with your friends!

Presentation can make as big an impression on your guests as flavor. Serving food on plain white dishes will allow the tasters to really stand out, but you can also utilize cutting boards, cocktail napkins, glasses, or spoons to display tasters of various shapes and sizes. Garnish dishes with a drizzle of sauce, a fruit or vegetable carved into an interesting shape, or edible flowers such as nasturtiums or violets.

You don't have to do all the preparation yourself! Give your friends a chance to show off their culinary prowess by bringing a dish to share. Be sure to have extra serving dishes and oven space available in case guests bring food that needs to be plated or warmed up before serving.

Most importantly, when planning and preparing a tasting party, have fun! Be creative and enjoy yourself.

Cocktail Party Offerings

Lobster and Fruit Cocktails

MAKES 8 TO 10 SERVINGS.

Ingredients

7 ounces (approximately 1 ½ cups or the meat of a 1 ¾ pound lobster) cooked and chopped lobster meat

½ cup cocktail sauce (store bought or homemade, see page 7)

⅔ cup frozen berries and fruit (such as blackberries, raspberries, blueberries, mango, and/or pineapple)

2 teaspoons lemon juice

Whole fresh strawberries

Directions

Mix fruit, lobster, and cocktail sauce. Place evenly into mini cocktail glasses. Garnish with fresh strawberries.

Mini Lobster Rolls

MAKES 10 TO 12 SERVINGS.

Ingredients

7 ounces (approximately 1 ½ cups or the meat of a 1 ¾ pound lobster) lobster meat, cooked and chopped.

4 teaspoons mayonnaise

2 teaspoons lemon juice

2-3 fresh cilantro sprigs, diced

Fresh cracked pepper to taste

1 diced green onion (optional)

Baguette

Directions

1. In a bowl, mix all the ingredients.
2. Slice baguette into 2-inch thick slices. Carefully scoop out middle of baguette slices, making a bread "cup." Fill each bread cup with the lobster salad.

Shrimp Cocktail Glasses

Ingredients

Large cooked and peeled shrimp (quantity can be any amount you desire)

Cocktail sauce (store bought or homemade, see below)
Cilantro sprigs
Lemon wedges

Directions

1. Fill cocktail glass ⅓ full with cocktail sauce and place three shrimp (or whatever number fits) around rim.
2. Garnish with cilantro sprigs. Serve with lemon wedges.

HOMEMADE COCKTAIL SAUCE

MAKES ABOUT 1 CUP (ENOUGH FOR ABOUT 2 POUNDS OF SHRIMP).

Ingredients

1 cup ketchup
1 tablespoon horseradish
1 teaspoon chili powder
1-2 tablespoon lemon or lime juice

1 teaspoon Worcestershire sauce
¼ teaspoon salt
¼ teaspoon pepper
¼ teaspoon cayenne

Directions

1. Combine all ingredients and stir.
2. If desired, adjust spices to make it as tangy and spicy as you like it.
3. Chill for at least two hours before serving.

Avocado Shrimp Cups

Ingredients

1 box filo shells (15 count)   Guacamole (see recipe on page 65)
15 small (50-70 count) cooked and
   peeled shrimp

Directions
1. Bake filo shells per directions on box. Drop a spoonful of guacamole in each shell.
2. Place one shrimp, tail removed, in each shell.
3. Garnish with cilantro sprig.

Fruit Kabobs

Ingredients

Cantaloupe, watermelon, strawberries, grapes, bananas, pineapple,
oranges, or any other fruits you like

Directions

1. Cut fruits into cubes or slices and skewer.
2. Serve with yogurt dipping sauce.

YOGURT DIPPING SAUCE

Ingredients

3 ounces cream cheese
⅓ cup brown sugar, packed

½ teaspoon vanilla
1 cup plain yogurt

Directions

1. In a small mixer bowl, combine cream cheese, brown sugar, and vanilla. Mix on medium speed until fluffy. Add yogurt and mix until smooth.
2. Serve in a small bowl near the fruit skewers.

> **Display Ideas!** Short on time? Skip the kabobs and simply slice or dice the fruit and arrange it on trays. Serve with figs, cheese and crackers, and the yogurt dipping sauce. Or, for a fun way to display your skewers, stick them in watermelon rind and set on a tray! You can also get creative with carving melon rinds into interesting designs for decoration.

Satay Chicken Skewers

Ingredients

¼ cup peanut butter

2 tablespoons finely chopped red onion

2 tablespoons finely chopped parsley

2 tablespoons fresh lemon juice (approximately ½ lemon)

1 ½ teaspoons soy sauce

1 teaspoon pepper sauce

3 tablespoons coconut milk (water, milk, or soy milk can be substituted)

1 pound boneless skinless chicken breasts

Directions

1. Combine all ingredients except chicken in a blender and blend until thoroughly combined. Place half of the sauce in a covered container and refrigerate.

2. Slice chicken into strips, ¼-to ½-inch thick. Place in remaining sauce and mix so all chicken is covered. Let marinate in refrigerator for 2 hours.

To cook:

Remove chicken from refrigerator. If you wish, you can skewer the chicken using either metal or wooden skewers. (If using wooden skewers, soak them in water first so they don't catch fire!)

The chicken is best if cooked on a grill or cast iron grill pan, though a standard skillet will also work. Heat grill/pan to medium-high heat. Once surface is heated, place chicken strip on, making sure not to overlap pieces. Cook on one side 4 to 5 minutes, flip, and cook an additional 3 to 4 minutes, or until chicken is no longer pink.

Serve with sauce you set aside from before. (Do not use leftover sauce that the chicken was marinating in!)

Bacon-Wrapped Dates with Maple Sauce

Ingredients

20 dates

9 bacon strips, sliced in half

1 tablespoon butter

½ can coconut milk

⅛ cup maple syrup

1 tablespoon flour

½ teaspoon salt

⅛ cup water

Directions

1. Wrap 18 dates (set two aside for use in the sauce) in bacon and skewer each with a toothpick. Place on baking sheet. Bake in pre-heated, 350 degree oven for 20-25 minutes or until bacon is crisp. Remove and let cool about 10 minutes before serving.

2. While dates are cooking, prepare sauce.

3. Cut two dates in half. Saute in butter until butter browns slightly. Add coconut milk and maple syrup. Let simmer 10 minutes. Remove from heat and take out date halves.

4. Mix flour and salt in ⅛ cup cold water until dissolved. Mix with coconut-maple sauce to thicken. If sauce is still runny, return to heat and simmer until thickened.

If you're a serious coconut lover, roll dates in coconut flakes before wrapping in bacon.

Ravioli

Dough:

2 ½ cups all-purpose flour

2 eggs

2 tablespoons olive oil

½ teaspoon salt

Directions

1. Mound flour in center of a large cutting board or cooking sheet and make a well in the top. Crack one egg and drop into well. Stir by hand slowly so egg and flour mix. Once one egg is mixed, add second egg. Mix in olive oil and salt until all ingredients are thoroughly combined.

2. To make ravioli, you can either use a ravioli maker, or make them by hand.

3. Roll out dough to about ⅛-inch thickness. Cut to desired size. Add dollop of filling to center of dough section. Cover with another dough section and crimp edges with fork. Drop finished ravioli into boiling water. Cook about 3 minutes or until they float. Once the ravioli float to the surface, they're done.

TOMATO SAUCE

Ingredients

2 pounds plum tomatoes
½ cup water
½ teaspoon rosemary
½ teaspoon basil
½ teaspoon marjoram
¼ teaspoon oregano
¼ teaspoon thyme

⅛ teaspoon red pepper
2 teaspoons sugar
2 teaspoons salt
1 ½ teaspoon pepper
¼ cup diced onion
2 tablespoons olive oil or butter

Directions

1. Dice tomatoes, leaving skin on. Put in pot with water on low heat. Cover and let simmer about 20 minutes, stirring every few minutes to avoid burning. Tomatoes will begin to break down.

2. While tomatoes are simmering, saute onions in oil or butter until soft.

3. Add onions and remaining ingredients to simmering tomatoes. Let simmer additional 10 minutes, stirring every few minutes.

4. Remove from heat. If chunky sauce is desired, you're done! If smoother sauce in desired, puree with food processor or stick blender.

Fried Ravioli

Ingredients

Olive oil, for frying

1 cup buttermilk

2 cups Italian-style breadcrumbs

¼ cup freshly grated Parmesan

Directions

1. Pour 2 inches olive oil into a large frying pan and heat over medium heat. If you have a deep-fry thermometer, it should register 325 degrees F.

2. While the oil is heating, put the buttermilk and the breadcrumbs in separate shallow bowls. Working in batches, dip pre-made ravioli in buttermilk to coat completely. Allow the excess buttermilk to drip back into the bowl. Dredge ravioli in the breadcrumbs. Place the ravioli on a baking sheet, and continue with the remaining ravioli.

3. When the oil is hot, fry the ravioli in batches, turning occasionally, until golden brown, about 3 minutes. Using a slotted spoon, transfer the fried ravioli to paper towels to drain.

4. Sprinkle the fried ravioli with Parmesan and serve with a bowl of warmed marinara sauce for dipping.

Homemade Crackers

Ingredients

1 ⅓ cups white flour

⅔ cup rye flour

1 teaspoon salt

½ teaspoon baking soda

⅓ cup oil

1 ½ tablespoons caraway seed

2 tablespoons vinegar

½ cup water

Directions

1. Preheat oven to 375 degrees.
2. Combine flours, salt, and baking soda. Add salt, caraway seeds, vinegar, and water. Mix well.
3. Roll out half of dough on a greased cookie sheet until it's an even ⅛-to ¼-inch thickness.
4. Score lightly and sprinkle with salt.
5. Bake 10 to 15 minutes until brown.
6. Repeat with remaining dough.

Cheese Platter

This is one of the easiest things you can prepare for a get-together. Simply buy a variety of cheeses (hard cheeses like cheddar, Swiss, Parmigiano-Reggiano, and soft cheese like Brie or feta). Slice hard cheese and place on a platter. Plate soft cheese with knives for spreading. You can also buy blocks or partial wheels of cheese and leave them on a cutting board with a knife for guests to help themselves. Garnish with grapes or berries and jams or apple slices sprinkled with lemon juice (to prevent browning).

Baked Brie

Ingredients

1 round or wedge of Brie cheese
    (leave rind on cheese)
Blackberry jam

Maple syrup (optional)
Aluminum foil

Directions

1. Preheat oven to 350 degrees.
2. Wrap Brie in aluminum foil and bake for 10 minutes.
3. Unwrap from foil and transfer to serving tray or baked tortilla.
4. Dollop blackberry jam onto Brie or drizzle with maple syrup. Serve with sliced bread, crackers, grapes, or apple slices.

> For a more elegant dish, dollop jam on Brie, then wrap Brie in puff pastry before cooking. Bake at 350 for 20 to 25 minutes.

Bruschetta with Tomato and Basil

Ingredients

1 baguette, sliced on a diagonal
Tomato-Basil Topping
6 or 7 ripe plum tomatoes (about 1
   ½ pounds)
1 tablespoon extra virgin olive oil,
   plus a little extra

2 tablespoons lemon juice
6-8 fresh basil leaves, finely chopped
¼ cup diced red onion
Salt and freshly ground black
   pepper to taste

Directions

1. Preheat oven to 450 degrees. Brush one side of bread slices with olive oil and place olive oil side down on a cookie sheet. Place baguette slices on a cookie sheet and toast on the top rack of your oven for 5 to 7 minutes, or until the bread is crisp and starts to brown.

2. Dice tomatoes and mix with olive oil and lemon juice.

3. Add chopped basil and onion and mix. Add salt and pepper to taste.

4. Put about a tablespoon of topping on each bread slice and arrange on a cutting board or platter to serve.

Bruschetta with Eggplant and Goat Cheese

Ingredients

1 baguette, sliced on a diagonal	1 eggplant
Tomato-Basil Topping	1 4-ounce package goat cheese
(see page 23)	2 ounces shredded mozzarella

Directions

1. Preheat oven to 450 degrees. Brush one side of baguette slices with olive oil and place olive oil side down on a cookie sheet. Place on the top rack of your oven and toast for 5 to 7 minutes, or until the bread is crisp and starts to brown. Remove from oven but leave on cookie sheet.

2. Thinly slice eggplant and saute lightly in olive oil.

3. Spread goat cheese on toasted baguette slices. Place one piece of eggplant on top of each, and then 1 tablespoon of tomato-basil topping. Sprinkle mozzarella on top.

4. Return cookie sheet to oven and bake for another 4 to 6 minutes or until cheese is melted.

Cheese-Stuffed Dates

Ingredients

3 tablespoons orange juice

½ cup crumbled blue cheese

2 ½ ounces cream cheese

½ cup chopped nuts (macadamia, pecans, or walnuts work best); set aside ¼ cup

20 pitted dates

Directions

1. Combine all ingredients, except ¼ cup chopped nuts.
2. Cover and refrigerate at least an hour.
3. Stuff each date with a heaping spoonful of the mixture. Slice date open on top if pit hole isn't large enough.
4. Top with remaining nuts.

For a simpler variation, stuff dates with pieces of hard cheese (cheddar, Parmesan, or your favorite), or with roasted nuts (macadamia, almond, etc.).

Cherry Tomato Caprese

Ingredients

Cherry tomatoes

Low-moisture mozzarella

Basil

Olive oil

Balsamic vinegar

Directions

Slice cherry tomatoes in half. De-seed if desired. Remove stems from tomatoes. Slice pieces of mozzarella about ½-inch thick and cut pieces to size of tomatoes. Place one slice in each tomato along with a basil leaf. Skewer with toothpick and place on serving dish. Put olive oil and balsamic in two dipping saucers so guests may dip as desired.

Sliced Flank Steak Crostini with Horseradish Sauce

Ingredients

2 ½- to 3-pound flank steak   Salt and pepper
Olive oil

Directions

1. Position a rack in the center of the oven and heat oven to 375 degrees.
2. Place steak on a baking sheet and rub with olive oil. Season with salt and pepper.
3. Bake at 375 for 15 minutes, then then switch to broil on high for 4 minutes.
4. Flip and broil another 4 minutes.
5. Remove and let rest 10 minutes.
6. This will render meat a medium-rare.
7. Slice beef thinly on platter. Serve with sliced baguette or crostini and horseradish sauce.

HORSERADISH SAUCE

Ingredients

2 tablespoons horseradish   3 tablespoons mayonnaise
1 tablespoon apple cider vinegar   ⅛ teaspoon ground red pepper
1 teaspoon ground mustard seed   ½ cup sour cream

Directions

Combine all ingredients in a bowl and whisk smooth. Chill before serving.

Chicken Salad Lettuce Cups

Ingredients

1 boneless, skinless chicken breast

1 tablespoon mayonnaise

1 tablespoon chopped pecans

1 tablespoon chopped dried cranberries

Salt and pepper to taste

¼ (a wedge) iceberg lettuce

Directions

1. Poach chicken breast: Place in a saucepan and add water so that it covers the chicken by at least half an inch. Bring to a boil, reduce heat, cover pot, and simmer for about 10 minutes. Turn off the heat and allow chicken to keep cooking in hot water for another 10 to 15 minutes.

2. Remove chicken from poaching water and dice. Mix with mayonnaise, chopped pecans, chopped cranberries, and salt and pepper.

3. Fill individual leaves of lettuce with chicken salad. If lettuce cups are sagging, skewer with a toothpick to hold in place.

4. This will make a variety of shapes/sizes and should yield around 6-8 servings.

Prosciutto-Wrapped Melon

Ingredients

Honeydew melon, cantaloupe, or both

Prosciutto

Directions

1. Cut melon into cubes or slices, or use a melon baller to scoop balls out.
2. Cut prosciutto into strips.
3. Wrap strips of prosciutto around melon and skewer melon with toothpick.
4. Serve arranged on a platter.

> You can also add a square of mozzarella to the end of the skewer or serve with a yogurt dipping sauce. Also, try wrapping grilled asparagus instead of melon!

Cool Yogurt Shrimp

Ingredients

½ cup nonfat plain yogurt

¼ cup reduced-fat sour cream

¼ cup chopped fresh chives

¼ cup chopped fresh tarragon

2 teaspoons Dijon mustard

1 teaspoon olive oil

2 teaspoons sugar

½ teaspoon salt

¼ teaspoon freshly ground black pepper

2 medium lemons

1 pound cooked shrimp (any size)

Directions

Place yogurt, sour cream, chives, tarragon, mustard, oil, sugar, salt, and pepper in a bowl. Zest lemons over bowl. Juice 1 lemon, making sure to catch seeds. Add juice to bowl. Stir until smooth. Add shrimp. Toss to coat and serve with remaining lemon, cut into wedges, if desired.

To make this a complete meal, serve over a bed of greens or cooked noodles.

Spiced Nuts

Ingredients

½ teaspoon ground cumin

½ teaspoon chili powder

½ teaspoon curry powder

¼ teaspoon cayenne pepper

¼ teaspoon powdered ginger

¼ teaspoon ground cinnamon

2 tablespoons olive oil

2 cups shelled nuts (include peanuts, walnuts, almonds, macadamia nuts, Brazil nuts, or any of your favorites)

1 tablespoon coarse salt (optional)

Directions

1. Preheat oven to 325 degrees.
2. In a bowl, mix cumin, chili powder, curry powder, cayenne, ginger, and cinnamon.
3. Heat oil in a nonstick skillet over low heat. Add spice mixture and stir well. Simmer for 3 to 4 minutes to mellow flavors.
4. Place nuts in a bowl. Add spice mixture onto nuts (scrape from skillet if necessary) and toss well. Spread nuts in one layer on a baking sheet.
5. Bake for 15 minutes, shaking the pan several times during baking.
6. Remove from oven.
7. If desired, sprinkle with coarse salt.
8. Let rest for 2 hours in a cool place. Store in airtight jars, or pack up as gifts.

Sugar-Glazed Nuts

Ingredients

½ cup butter

1 cup brown sugar

1 teaspoon cinnamon

4 cups nuts (any variety)

Directions

1. Preheat oven to 325 degrees.
2. Spread nuts in one layer on a baking sheet.
3. Roast in oven 10 to 15 minutes, until lightly browned.
4. Remove and let cool.
5. While cooling, melt butter over medium-low heat in skillet.
6. Stir in brown sugar and cinnamon.
7. Saute ingredients 3 to 5 minutes, until dissolved in butter.
8. Add nuts. Stir to coat all nuts and saute another 3 to 5 minutes. Remove from heat.
9. Spread over wax paper and let cool.

Sauteed Pear Slices with Pancetta and Gorgonzola

Ingredients

12 thin slices pancetta (about ⅓ pound)

2 pears (Bartlett are best, but most will work fine)

2 tablespoons butter

2 tablespoons sugar

4 ounces gorgonzola cheese, crumbled

Freshly cracked pepper

Honey or maple syrup for drizzling

Directions

1. Saute pancetta in a skillet until lightly browned and just starting to crisp.
2. Core pears with an apple corer and slice into 12 thin rings.
3. In skillet, melt butter and sugar together until it begins to caramelize.
4. Saute pear slices in sugar sauce. Remove and set slices on plates.
5. Top each slice with pancetta and gorgonzola.
6. Crack fresh pepper over the top and drizzle with honey or maple syrup.
7. Garnish with fresh thyme sprigs if desired.

Mini Quiches

Ingredients

12 slices of bread
1 onion, grated
½ cup shredded Swiss cheese
¼ cup sliced ham, cut into squares
¼ cup broccoli, diced

1 cup milk
4 eggs
1 teaspoon mustard powder
Salt and pepper to taste

Directions

1. Preheat oven to 375 degrees.
2. Lightly grease 12 muffin tins.
3. Trim or cut bread into circles. Place circles in bottom of muffin tins. Distribute the onion and shredded cheese evenly between the muffin tins.
4. In a medium bowl, combine remaining ingredients.
5. Divide between the muffin tins.
6. Bake in preheated oven for 20 minutes, or until a toothpick inserted into the center of a quiche comes out clean.

Toasted Apple Spinach Brie Bites

Ingredients

1 loaf French bread

3 medium honey crisp apples (or your favorite variety), sliced

1 wedge brie cheese

Baby spinach

1 pound sliced turkey

Directions

1. Preheat oven to 350 degrees.
2. Slice loaf in half, lengthwise.
3. Toast bread in a preheated oven until lightly browned.
4. Remove and let cool.
5. Once bread is cool, layer spinach, apples, turkey, and brie. If desired, you can spread mayonnaise or mustard on the bread as well.
6. Wrap sandwich in aluminum foil and bake for 10 minutes in 350 degree oven to heat sandwich and let cheese melt slightly.
7. Remove, slice, and serve!

Mini Muffins

Ingredients

1 ½ cups all-purpose flour

¾ cup white sugar

½ teaspoon salt

2 teaspoons baking powder

⅓ cup vegetable oil

1 egg

⅓ cup milk

1 cup fresh blueberries

Directions:

1. Preheat oven to 350 degrees.
2. Line mini muffin pan with liners or grease each cup.
3. Combine 1 ½ cups flour, ¾ cup sugar, salt, and baking powder.
4. Combine oil, egg, and milk in a bowl and mix lightly to combine.
5. Mix this with flour mixture.
6. Fold in blueberries.
7. Fill muffin cups right to the top.
8. Bake 8 to 10 minutes.
9. Muffins are done when tops have rounded up and a toothpick inserted comes out clean.

Baked Caramelized Onion and Goat Cheese Quesadillas

MAKES 8-16 WEDGES, DEPENDING ON HOW YOU CUT THE WEDGES

Ingredients

4 (10-inch) flour tortillas

1 red onion, thinly sliced

1 tablespoon brown sugar

¼ teaspoon balsamic vinegar

1 ½ cups goat cheese

2 tablespoons butter

Directions

Onions

1. Melt 2 tablespoons butter in a skillet over medium heat.
2. Add onion, brown sugar, and vinegar.
3. Saute until onion is golden brown, stirring frequently, about 25 minutes.
4. Remove from heat and let cool to room temperature.

Quesadillas

1. Preheat oven to 350 degrees.
2. Place two tortillas on a baking sheet.
3. Sprinkle cheese over tortillas.
4. Divide sauteed onions evenly over tortillas. Season with salt and pepper if desired.
5. Place other tortillas on top.
6. Bake until golden, about 10 minutes.
7. Remove and cut into wedges.

Game Day Snacks

Chicken Wings

Ingredients

12 wing sections	Oil for frying

Directions

1. Fry wings in 350 degree oil for 10 to 15 minutes. Make sure chicken is cooked through (chicken should not be pink on the inside).
2. Remove and place on paper towels to allow excess oil to soak up.
3. Toss in a bowl with sauce of choice (see below and on following pages).

ASIAN FUSION SAUCE

Ingredients

¼ cup soy sauce	¼ cup lemon juice
½ cup water	1 ½ teaspoons fresh grated ginger
1 ½ teaspoons crushed red pepper	2 tablespoons flour
¼ cup sugar	

Directions

1. Combine all ingredients except flour in saucepan and heat over medium heat, stirring to avoid burning. Simmer 10 minutes.
2. Combine flour in 1/8 cup cold water and stir until smooth. Add to sauce and simmer another 3-5 minutes while stirring to thicken. If desired, strain sauce to remove pepper flakes.

SPICY MAPLE SAUCE

Ingredients

¼ cup real maple syrup (no substitutes!)	1 teaspoon crushed red pepper
	½ teaspoon salt
½ cup water	2 tablespoons flour

Continued on page 49

Directions

1. Combine all ingredients except flour in saucepan and heat over medium heat, stirring to avoid burning. Simmer 10 minutes.

2. Combine flour in ⅛ cup cold water and stir until smooth. Add to sauce and simmer another 3-5 minutes while stirring to thicken. If desired, strain sauce to remove pepper flakes.

> For a slightly stronger flavor, shake some smokehouse maple seasoning or a little brown sugar into the sauce.

BUFFALO SAUCE

Ingredients

¼ cup (1 stick) butter, melted

½ cup of your favorite hot sauce

1-2 teaspoons white vinegar, optional

A little corn starch, flour, or xantham gum to thicken sauce

Directions

1. On medium-low heat, melt butter. Stir in hot sauce, vinegar, and thickening agent. Mix wings while sauce is still hot.

> Shake some mesquite into sauce for a slightly fuller flavor. Serve with blue cheese dressing (see recipe below).

BLUE CHEESE DRESSING

Mix together:

6 ounces blue cheese, crumbled

1 small onion, peeled and diced

1 cup mayonnaise

¼ cup ketchup

¼ cup olive oil

2 tablespoons apple cider vinegar

½ teaspoon paprika

½ teaspoon salt

½ teaspoon Dijon mustard

⅛ teaspoon cayenne pepper

Cookie Cutter Pizzas

PIZZA DOUGH

Ingredients

1 package (2 ¼ teaspoons) dry yeast

1 cup warm water

3 cups flour

1 teaspoon sugar

1 ½ teaspoons salt

¼ cup olive oil

PIZZA SAUCE

Ingredients

1 6-ounce can tomato paste

¼ cup water

¼ teaspoon sugar

½ teaspoon salt

½ teaspoon pepper

1 ½ teaspoon Italian seasoning

Directions

1. Dissolve yeast in warm water.
2. Add sugar, salt, and oil; mix thoroughly.
3. Add ½ of the flour and beat until there are no lumps remaining.
4. Gradually add remaining flour.
5. Knead dough for 5 minutes.
6. Put in bowl, cover with moistened towel/paper towels and allow to rise 20 to 30 minutes.
7. Roll out to about ¼" thickness and transfer to a greased cookie sheet.
8. Bake at 450 degrees until dough starts to brown, then remove.
9. Let cool.
10. Use cookie cutters to cut out shapes, cutting each shape as close as possible to the next to avoid wasted dough.
11. Add sauce, cheese, and toppings of your choice.
12. Bake again at 450 degrees for 10 minutes, until cheese is golden brown.

Beef Sliders

Ingredients

1 pound high-quality ground beef (such as Kobe)

1 ½ teaspoons onion powder

1 ½ teaspoons salt

1 teaspoon freshly ground black pepper

2 shallots, finely chopped

12 slider buns (such as Hawaiian sweet rolls)

Sliced cheese of your choice

Small leaf greens, tomato, onion, pickles

Condiments of your choice (ketchup, mustard, mayonnaise, relish, etc.)

Directions

1. Start up your grill so it can heat while you're mixing the beef and seasonings.

2. In a medium-sized mixing bowl, add the beef, seasonings, and shallots. Mix the meat with your hands, thoroughly incorporating the seasonings and shallots.

3. Form the meat into small-sized patties.

4. Grill the patties for 2 to 3 minutes per side.

5. If you wish, top each patty with a slice of cheese for the last two minutes and allow it to start melting. When the cheese has melted, remove the patties from grill.

6. Serve on the rolls, allowing guests to garnish as they wish.

7. Toast or grill the rolls if desired.

Pulled Pork Sliders

MAKES 20 SLIDERS

Ingredients

1 teaspoon vegetable oil

1 pork shoulder roast (about 4 pounds)

1 cup barbeque sauce

½ cup apple cider vinegar

½ cup chicken broth

¼ cup light brown sugar

1 tablespoon prepared yellow mustard

1 tablespoon Worcestershire sauce

1 tablespoon chili powder

1 extra large onion (chopped)

1 ½ teaspoons dried thyme

20 slider buns

Coleslaw

1 small head cabbage (shredded)

3 medium carrots (shredded)

1 cup mayonnaise

⅓ cup sugar

¼ cup apple cider vinegar

Directions

1. Pour the vegetable oil into the bottom of the slow cooker. Put the pork roast into the slow cooker and pour in the barbeque sauce, apple cider vinegar, and chicken broth. Stir in brown sugar, mustard, Worcestershire sauce, chili powder, onion, and thyme.

2. Cover and cook on high for 5 to 6 hours or until the meat shreds easily with a fork.

3. Take the roast out of the slow cooker and shred using two forks. Place the shredded meat back into the slow cooker and stir with the juices. Let marinade while you prepare the coleslaw.

4. In a large bowl combine shredded cabbage and carrots. In a small bowl combine mayonnaise, sugar, and vinegar. Mix well and pour over the cabbage mixture, tossing to coat.

5. Assemble sliders, toasting or grilling buns if desired.

Grilled Veggie Sliders

MAKES 8 SLIDERS

Ingredients

4 plum tomatoes	⅛ cup balsamic vinegar
2 small zucchini	⅛ cup extra virgin olive oil
1 medium green pepper	½ cup shredded mozzarella cheese
1 medium onion	Salt and pepper to taste
1 8 ounce package mushrooms	6 slider rolls

Directions

1. Slice the vegetables and place together in a bowl. Add half the oil and vinegar and toss to coat.
2. Saute in skillet over medium-high heat until vegetables are tender, about 15 minutes, stirring occasionally while they saute.
3. Remove the vegetables to a large bowl. Add the remaining oil and vinegar. Stir in the cheese.
4. Split the rolls and grill until toasted.
5. Divide the vegetable medley among the buns.
6. Add salt and pepper to taste.

Bacon-Wrapped Jalapeños

MAKES 20

Ingredients

10 whole fresh jalapenos, each 2 to 3 inches long

1 block (8 ounces) cream cheese, softened

10 strips bacon, sliced in half

Directions

1. Preheat oven to 375 degrees.
2. Cut jalapenos in half lengthwise.
3. With a spoon, remove the seeds and white membrane.
4. Spread softened cream cheese into each jalapeno half.
5. Wrap jalapeno with bacon pieces (½ slice per pepper) and secure by sticking toothpick through the middle.
6. Bake on a pan with a rack for 20 to 25 minutes, until bacon is crispy.

You may want to wear latex gloves while cutting the peppers, as the acid from them can irritate bare skin.

Fried Stuffed Jalapeños

Directions

Heat deep fryer to 350, or heat oil in frying pan to medium-high. While oil is heating, prepare jalapenos as described for bacon-wrapped jalapenos, except don't wrap with bacon. If desired, you can stuff them with cheddar or mozzarella instead of cream cheese.

In one bowl: Mix 1 egg with ½ cup milk. Mix thoroughly.
In second bowl: Place ½ cup flour.
In third bowl: Place ½ cup bread crumbs.

After stuffing jalapenos, dredge in flour. Shake off excess flour. Dip in egg mix. Roll in bread crumbs and place on a plate. Once all jalapenos are coated, place in hot oil. Cook about 3 minutes, until golden brown.

For added flavor, mix cream cheese with a little crab meat, shallots, or cooked ground sausage.

Homemade Corn Chips

Ingredients

1 cup cornmeal

1 tablespoon corn oil

½ teaspoon salt

¾ cup boiling water

Extra cornmeal for rolling

Directions

1. Mix all ingredients.
2. Roll out to ⅛-inch thickness on well-greased baking sheet.
3. Bake in 400 degree oven for about 10 minutes.
4. Remove and let cool. Break into chips.

To make triangles, cut rolled-out dough into wedges using a pizza cutter or butter knife. (Don't press so hard that you scratch your cookie sheet.)

Potato Chips

Ingredients

4 medium potatoes (1½–2 pounds), sliced paper-thin (peels are optional; use a mandolin or food processor with thin slicer for best and easiest results)

3 tablespoons salt

Vegetable or peanut oil for frying

Directions

1. Place potato slices into a large bowl of cold water as you slice.
2. Drain and rinse. Refill the bowl with water and add the salt.
3. Let the potatoes soak in the salty water for at least 30 minutes.
4. Drain, then rinse, and drain again.
5. Lay potatoes out on paper towels to absorb excess water.
6. Heat oil in a deep fryer to 365 degrees.
7. Fry potato slices in small batches.
8. Once they start turning golden, remove and drain on paper towels.
9. Continue until all of the slices are fried.

Serve as plain potato chips; season with additional salt, or dust with mesquite, cayenne, or other favorite flavorings; or toss in a bowl with a little malt vinegar.

Sweet Potato or Root Vegetable Chips

Ingredients

2 pounds sweet potatoes, parsnips, beets, or other root vegetables, thinly sliced (use a mandolin or food processor with thin slicer for best and easiest results)

Vegetable or peanut oil for frying
1 teaspoon cinnamon
¼ cup sugar

Directions

1. Place potato slices into a large bowl of cold water as you slice.
2. Drain and rinse. Lay out on paper towels to absorb excess water.
3. Heat oil in a deep fryer to 365 degrees.
4. Fry potato slices in small batches.
5. Once they start turning golden, remove and drain on paper towels.
6. Continue until all of the slices are fried.
7. Combine sugar and cinnamon and sprinkle over chips.

For a simple but impressive spread, make one or two homemade treats (like these chips) and serve with a cold-cut platter. Arrange a selection of sliced meats (ham, turkey, roast beef, salami, etc.) on a serving platter. Serve with crackers or bread and cheese. Supplement with a crudite tray and homemade dips (see page 68) or a selection of olives.

Guacamole

Ingredients

2 ripe avocados

8 cilantro leaves, finely chopped

½ lime, juiced

1 ¼ inch wide slice of jalapeno, diced and crushed to allow juices to release

Salt and pepper

Directions

Mash avocado in a bowl. Add cilantro, lime juice, and jalapeno. Mix. Add salt and pepper to taste.

If desired, add 1 medium tomato, diced, or more jalapeno or hot sauce for an extra kick.

Guacamole Roja

Ingredients

1 ripe avocado

¼ cup tomato salsa

¼ cup sour cream

Hot sauce to taste

Salt and pepper to taste

Directions

Mash avocado in bowl. Add salsa and sour cream and mix. Add hot sauce and salt and pepper to taste.

Soft Pretzels with Dipping Sauces

Ingredients

4 teaspoons active dry yeast

1 teaspoon white sugar

1 ¼ cups warm water

5 cups all-purpose flour

½ cup white sugar

1 ½ teaspoons salt

1 tablespoon vegetable oil

½ cup baking soda

4 cups hot water

¼ cup kosher salt, for topping

Directions

1. In a small bowl, dissolve yeast and 1 teaspoon sugar in warm water.
2. Let stand until creamy, about 10 minutes.
3. In a large bowl, mix together flour, ½ cup sugar, and salt.
4. Make a well in the center; add the oil and yeast mixture.
5. Mix and form into a dough. (If the mixture is dry, add one or two tablespoons of water.)
6. Knead the dough until smooth.
7. Lightly oil a large bowl and place the dough in the bowl. Turn to coat evenly with oil.
8. Cover with plastic wrap and let rise in a warm place until doubled in size, about 1 hour.
9. Preheat oven to 450 degrees.
10. In a large bowl, dissolve baking soda in hot water.
11. When risen, turn dough out onto a lightly floured surface and divide into 12 equal pieces.
12. Roll each piece into a rope and twist into a pretzel shape.
13. Dip each pretzel into the baking soda solution and place on a greased baking sheet sprinkle with kosher salt.
14. Bake in preheated oven for 8 minutes, until browned.
15. Serve plain, or with mustard, cheese sauce, or other favorite dip.

CHEESE SAUCE FOR PRETZELS

Ingredients

2 tablespoons butter

2 tablespoons all-purpose flour

1 teaspoon salt

1 cup milk

1 cup shredded cheddar cheese

1 teaspoon mustard

Salt and pepper to taste

Directions

1. In a medium-size saucepan, melt butter.
2. Mix in flour and 1 teaspoon of salt.
3. Stir continually until the mixture is simmering.
4. Slowly pour milk into the mixture.
5. Continue stirring over a medium heat until the mixture has thickened.
6. Stir in cheese and mustard.
7. Continue stirring until all of the cheese is melted and the dip is smooth.
8. Serve warm after adding salt and pepper to taste.

Make a pretzel tree! Do this by hanging pretzels on a mug rack, or make a "tree" out of a 2x2 piece of wood with dowels inserted into drill holes.

Taco Cups

Ingredients

1 pound ground beef, chicken,
    or turkey, seasoned with a
    prebought package, your own
    favorite seasonings, or Simple
    Taco Meat Seasoning, below
1 bag corn chip scoops
Shredded cheese

Diced tomato
Shredded lettuce
Salsa
Guacamole
Sour cream
Black olives

Directions

Assemble shells on tray. Fill each shell with meat, cheese, and other top-pings of your choice!

SIMPLE TACO MEAT SEASONING

1 tablespoon chili powder
¼ teaspoon onion powder
¼ teaspoon crushed red pepper
    flakes
¼ teaspoon dried oregano

½ teaspoon paprika
1 ½ teaspoons ground cumin
1 teaspoon sea salt
1 teaspoon black pepper

> If desired, place cheese in cups first and broil for a minute in the oven to melt slightly before adding other ingredients.

Bread Bowl Dips

These dips can be served right out of a bread bowl. Buy a round loaf of bread or use the recipe below to make your own. To make a bowl, slice off the top of the bread and hollow out. Cube up remaining bread and toast lightly to serve with dip. Fill bread with the dip of your choice!

BAKED SPINACH DIP

Ingredients

2 (8-ounce) packages cream cheese, softened

1 cup mayonnaise

1 (10-ounce) package frozen chopped spinach, thawed and squeezed dry

1 (4-ounce) cup shredded cheddar cheese

¼ cup chopped onion

Directions

1. In a large bowl, beat cream cheese and mayonnaise until blended. Stir in the spinach, cheese, onion, and dill. Cover and refrigerate at least 1 hour.
2. Preheat oven to 350 degrees.
3. Place dip into glass cooking dish. Bake at 350 for half an hour, until warmed through.
4. Remove and serve with toasted bread, corn chips, or veggies.

> You can bake this dip right in the bread bowl. Fill bread bowl with dip. Put bowl on cooking sheet and cover with foil. Bake at 350 for an hour, or until dip is warmed through.

Dried Beef Dip

Ingredients

¾ cup sour cream

½ cup mayonnaise

⅓ cup chopped fresh flat-leaf
   parsley

¼ cup chopped fresh chives

¼ teaspoon salt

¼ teaspoon black pepper

2 (5-ounce) jars dried beef, chopped

Directions

Combine all ingredients in a bowl and chill at least 2 hours.

Bread Bowl

Ingredients

½ ounce (2 packages) active dry yeast

2 ½ cups warm water (Not too hot as it will kill yeast. Around 110 degrees should do it.)

2 teaspoons salt

2 tablespoons vegetable oil

7 cups all-purpose flour

1 tablespoon cornmeal

1 egg white

1 tablespoon water

Directions

1. Dissolve yeast in warm water in a large bowl.
2. Let stand until creamy (about 10 minutes).
3. Add salt, oil, and 4 cups flour to the yeast mixture and mix well.
4. Stir in the remaining flour, ½ cup at a time, mixing with an electric mixer at medium speed to combine ingredients.
5. When the dough has pulled together, turn it out onto a lightly floured surface and knead until smooth and elastic, about 6 minutes.
6. Place the dough in the lightly oiled bowl, turning to coat with oil.
7. Cover with a damp cloth and let rise in a warm place until doubled in size (35 to 45 minutes).
8. Punch dough down, and divide into 8 equal portions.
9. Shape each portion into a 4-inch round loaf.
10. Lightly grease 2 baking sheets and sprinkle cornmeal on them.
11. Place loaves on baking sheets (2 per sheet).
12. Cover and let rise in a warm place until doubled in size again (35 to 45 minutes).
13. While dough is rising, preheat oven to 400 degrees.

14. In a small bowl, beat together egg white and 1 tablespoon water; lightly brush the loaves with half of this egg wash.
15. Bake in preheated oven for 15 minutes.
16. Brush with remaining egg mixture, and bake an additional 10 to 15 more minutes, until golden.
17. Cool on wire racks.

Cheese Quesadillas

Ingredients

2 (10-inch) flour tortillas

½ cup grated cheese (sharp cheddar or Mexican blend is best, but mozzarella is fine, too)

2 teaspoons butter

Salsa, sour cream, and guacamole for the side

Directions:

1. Heat skillet (large enough to fit tortillas) over medium-high heat.
2. Melt 1 teaspoon butter. Tilt skillet to coat entire surface area.
3. Place one tortilla in skillet, to allow butter to absorb into tortilla.
4. Remove and place, on a plate, butter side up.
5. Repeat first step.
6. Place second tortilla in skillet.
7. Sprinkle the cheese on tortilla in skillet.
8. Place other tortilla, butter side up, on cheese and tortilla in skillet.
9. Cook until cheese begins to melt (2 to 3 minutes or until golden brown).
10. Flip, and cook another 2 to 3 minutes (again, or until golden brown).
11. Remove, place on plate, and cut into wedges.
12. Serve with salsa, sour cream, and guacamole.

Kabobs

Ingredients

½ cup teriyaki sauce

½ cup honey

½ pinch ground ginger

1 red bell pepper, cut into 2-inch pieces

1 green bell pepper, cut into 2-inch pieces

1 large sweet onion, peeled and cut into wedges

1 ½ cups whole fresh mushrooms

1 pound beef sirloin, cut into 1-inch cubes

1 ½ pounds skinless, boneless chicken breast halves, cut into cubes

skewers

Directions

1. In large bowl, combine teriyaki sauce, honey, and ginger. Stir.
2. Add peppers, onions, mushrooms, beef, and chicken.
3. Seal, and refrigerate at least 4 hours.
4. Preheat grill for medium-high heat.
5. Thread the meat and vegetables onto skewers, leaving a small space between each item.
6. Lightly oil the grill grate.
7. Grill skewers for 10 minutes, turning as needed, or until meat is cooked through and vegetables are tender.

Black Bean Salsa

Ingredients

3 (15-ounce) cans black beans, drained and rinsed

1 (11-ounce) can whole kernel corn, drained

2 (10-ounce) cans diced tomatoes with green chili peppers, partially drained

2 plum tomatoes, diced

2 bunches green onions, chopped

5 fresh cilantro leaves, finely chopped (you may want a few more for garnish)

Salt and pepper

Directions

Mix all ingredients together in a large bowl. Garnish with desired amount of cilantro leaves. Add salt and pepper to taste. Refrigerate at least 8 hours before serving.

Potato Puffs

Ingredients

3 large baking potatoes

2 tablespoons butter

½ cup milk

¼ cup sour cream

½ cup shredded cheese (cheddar,

mozzarella, or Monterey jack)

1 green onion, diced

Salt and pepper to taste

Directions

1. Peel potatoes and cut into small pieces. Place in a large pot, cover with water, and bring to a boil. Cook for about 15 minutes or until potatoes are soft. Drain and mash potatoes.

2. Mix in other ingredients.

3. Scoop onto baking sheet using a melon baller or spoon 4.

4. Broil on high for 3 to 5 minutes, until golden brown.

Potato Skins

Ingredients

4 baking potatoes

½ cup shredded cheese

4 strips bacon (optional)

4 crowns cooked broccoli (optional)

2 green onions/chives

Sour cream and salsa to your liking

Directions

1. Clean potatoes.

2. Bake potatoes in oven or microwave. If in oven, preheat to 350, lightly coat with oil, and poke with fork eight or more times to allow moisture to escape while cooking. Place on lower rack. Bake 1 to 1 ½ hours, until skin is crisp and flesh inside is soft. If in microwave, prep the same as oven method, place in microwave, cook on high starting at 10 minutes. If more time is needed, continue for a minute or less at a time.

3. While potatoes are baking, cook bacon.

4. Once potatoes are baked, let cool to comfortable level, then cut in half lengthwise.

5. Scoop out flesh. Save flesh for other uses, such as mashed potatoes or fried potatoes.

6. If a crispier skin is desired, prebake skins at 450 for 10 minutes, then flip and bake 10 more.

7. Fill with shredded cheese and crumbled bacon and broccoli if desired.

8. Broil for 2 to 3 minutes, until cheese is bubbly and golden.

9. Remove and serve with sour cream, salsa, and chopped green onions/chives on the side.

Tomato Salsa

Ingredients

2 cups chopped tomatoes

1 jalapeno pepper, diced

5 fresh cilantro leaves, finely
  chopped

Dash of vinegar (optional)

Juice of one lemon

½ cup chopped red onion

1 tablespoon olive oil

Salt to taste

Directions

Combine all ingredients. Cover and chill at least 2 hours.

{ Mini Desserts }

Coconut Cake Bites

Ingredients

1 stick salted butter, at room temperature

1 cup sugar

2 eggs

1 ½ cups sifted self-rising flour

½ cup coconut milk

½ teaspoon pure vanilla extract

Directions

1. Preheat oven to 350 degrees.
2. Grease and flour three 9 x 9 inch cake pans.
3. Using an electric mixer, cream butter until fluffy. Add sugar and continue to cream well for 6 to 8 minutes.
4. Add eggs, one at a time, beating well after each addition.
5. Add flour and milk alternately to creamed mixture, beginning and ending with flour.
6. Add vanilla and continue to beat until just mixed.
7. Bake at 350 for 12 to 15 minutes, until cake is golden brown and toothpick inserted comes out clean. Cool completely before frosting.

FROSTING

Ingredients

4 ounces cream cheese, softened

½ stick unsalted butter, softened

2 cups confectioners' sugar

1 tablespoon heavy cream

¼ teaspoon salt

½ teaspoon vanilla extract

½ cup toasted coconut flakes for garnish

Directions

1. Slowly mix all ingredients in mixer until smooth.
2. Frost top of cake and slice into small squares.
3. Sprinkle with toasted coconut.

Chocolate-Dipped Strawberries

Ingredients

1 12-ounce bag semisweet chocolate chips

3 ounces white chocolate, chopped

1 pound strawberries with stems, washed and dried

1 tablespoon vegetable oil

Directions

1. Combine chocolate chips and oil in a double boiler. (If you don't have a double boiler, you can use a saucepan, but stir constantly to avoid burning the chocolate.) Melt over very low heat.

2. Once chocolate is melted to a smooth, velvety texture, remove from heat.

3. Dip strawberries one at a time and place on lightly greased or parchment-lined cookie sheet.

4. Refrigerate half an hour.

5. Once chocolate has set on strawberries, melt the white chocolate and drizzle over strawberries using a fork.

> For variety, dip other fruits and foods in chocolate, such as bananas, orange sections, macaroons, marshmallows, pretzel sticks, or dried apricots Or make clementine poppers by coating segments in chocolate and freezing.

Raspberry Sorbet

Ingredients

1 cup water

½ cup sugar

2 cups fresh raspberries

Juice of ½ lemon (around 2 tablespoons)

Directions

1. Combine all ingredients in a saucepan and bring to boil, stirring to avoid burning.
2. Boil 3 to 4 minutes.
3. Simmer additional 10 minutes, allowing raspberries to break down.
4. After mix cools, blend well with an immersion blender.
5. Strain through mesh strainer (or through colander lined with cheesecloth if you don't have a mesh strainer), pressing on the solids.
6. Chill puree for 1 hour or until cold, or quick chill in a bowl of ice and cold water, stirring occasionally for 15 to 20 minutes (until cold).
7. Freeze puree in ice-cream maker according to directions. Makes 1 pint.
8. Garnish with berries if desired.

You can substitute other fruits, such as strawberries or blueberries, for the raspberries. For a festive display, serve sorbet in a cracked coconut shell.

S'mores Bites

Ingredients

3 graham crackers

3 marshmallows

2 ounces milk chocolate

Directions

1. Break each graham cracker into four sections and place on a baking sheet.
2. Cut each marshmallow into four sections, lengthways.
3. Place one marshmallow section on each graham cracker piece.
4. Bake at 350 for 8 to 10 minutes, until marshmallows begin to brown. Remove and let cool.
5. Melt milk chocolate in a double boiler or saucepan over low heat.
6. Dip each s'more in chocolate and place on baking sheet lined with wax paper.
7. Refrigerate until chocolate sets.

MARSHMALLOWS

Ingredients

1 cup confectioners' sugar

3 ½ envelopes unflavored gelatin

1 cup cold water, divided

2 cups granulated sugar

½ cup light corn syrup

¼ teaspoon salt

2 large egg whites or reconstituted powdered egg whites

1 tablespoon vanilla (or ½ of a scraped vanilla bean or 2 teaspoons almond or mint extract)

Continued on page 92

Directions

1. Grease bottom and sides of a 13 x 9 x 2 inch rectangular metal baking pan and dust bottom and sides with confectioners' sugar.

2. In the bowl of a standing electric mixer or in a large bowl sprinkle gelatin over ½ cup cold water, and let stand to soften.

3. In a 3-quart heavy saucepan cook granulated sugar, corn syrup, second ½ cup of cold water, and salt over low heat, stirring with a wooden spoon, until sugar is dissolved. Increase heat to moderate and boil mixture, without stirring, until a candy or digital thermometer registers 240°F, about 12 minutes. Remove pan from heat and pour sugar mixture over gelatin mixture, stirring until gelatin is dissolved.

4. With a standing or a hand-held electric mixer beat mixture on high speed until white, thick, and nearly tripled in volume, about 6 minutes if using standing mixer or about 10 minutes if using hand-held mixer.

5. In separate medium bowl with cleaned beaters beat egg whites (or reconstituted powdered whites) until they just hold stiff peaks. Beat whites and vanilla (or your choice of flavoring) into sugar mixture until just combined. Pour mixture into baking pan. Sift ¼ cup confectioners' sugar evenly over top. Chill marshmallows, uncovered, until firm, at least 3 hours, and up to 1 day.

6. Run a thin knife around edges of pan and invert pan onto a large cutting board. Lifting up one corner of inverted pan, with fingers loosen marshmallow and ease onto cutting board. With a large knife trim edges of marshmallow and cut marshmallow into roughly 1-inch cubes. (An oiled pizza cutter works well here too.) Sift remaining confectioners' sugar back into your now-empty baking pan, and roll the marshmallows through it, on all six sides, before shaking off the excess and packing them away.

Graham Crackers

Ingredients

2 ½ cups all-purpose, unbleached flour (set aside a little extra for dusting)

1 cup lightly packed light brown sugar

1 teaspoon baking soda

¾ teaspoon salt

7 tablespoons unsalted butter, cut into cubes and chilled

⅓ cup honey

5 tablespoons milk

2 tablespoons pure vanilla extract

¼ cup granulated sugar

1 teaspoon ground cinnamon

Directions

1. Combine the flour, brown sugar, baking soda, and salt in a mixing bowl. Mix on low to combine all ingredients.
2. Add the butter and mix on low until the mixture resembles coarse meal.
3. In a small bowl, combine honey, milk, and vanilla. Stir.
4. Add to the flour mixture and mix on low until the dough starts to come together.
5. Place in refrigerator for 20 minutes to firm.
6. While dough is firming, mix the cinnamon and sugar in a bowl.
7. Divide the dough in half and roll out unto a lightly floured surface into a long rectangle, about an ⅛-inch thick. Flour as necessary to keep from sticking. Trim the edges to make the rectangle 8 inches wide and 12 inches long. From this, you can make six 4 x 4 inch graham crackers, giving them the traditional shape.
8. Bake at 350 degrees for 12 to 15 minutes, rotating halfway through.
9. Keep checking on them to make sure you don't burn the crackers. You will want them to be slightly firm to the touch.
10. Repeat with remaining dough.

Easy Fudge

Ingredients

3 cups semisweet chocolate chips

1 (14-ounce) can sweetened condensed milk

¼ cup butter

Directions

1. In a double boiler, combine chocolate chips and condensed milk. Melt over low heat, stirring to mix chocolate and milk thoroughly.

2. Once melted, pour into a well-greased glass baking dish. Refrigerate until set.

Variations: Stir chopped nuts, mini marshmallows, or other candies into mix (a combined total of about 1 cup for recipe). For peanut butter fudge, use peanut butter chips instead of chocolate. Or use white chocolate chips and add your flavor of choice!

Mini Sundaes

In tasting bowls, place small scoops of ice cream. Serve on a table with toppings in bowls to allow guests to create their sundaes of choice!

Topping ideas:

Hot fudge, caramel, marshmallow, cherries, whipped cream, mini chocolate chips, coconut flakes, sprinkles.

Chocolate Mousse Desserts

Ingredients

8 ounces semisweet chocolate (chips or coarsely chopped from squares)

½ cup water, divided in two

2 tablespoons butter

3 egg yolks

2 tablespoons sugar

1 ¼ cups whipping cream, whipped

Directions

1. In a double boiler, heat chocolate, ¼ cup water, and butter until the chocolate and butter are melted. Cool for 10 minutes.
2. In a small heavy saucepan, whisk egg yolks, sugar, and remaining water.
3. Cook and stir over low heat, about 1 to 2 minutes. (Mixture should reach around 160 degrees.)
4. Remove from the heat.
5. Whisk in chocolate mixture.
6. Set saucepan in ice and stir until cooled, about 5 to 10 minutes.
7. Fold in whipped cream.
8. Spoon into dessert dishes.
9. Refrigerate for at least 2 hours.

Chocolate Tasting

For a chocolate tasting party, plan to provide about ½ ounce of each type of chocolate per guest. Provide at least 4 to 6 kinds of chocolate, such as milk, dark, white, or varieties with nuts, berries, ginger bits, and so forth. Cut your bars into an assortment of sizes, some some small and others larger so guests can bite into the chocolate.

Serve with coffees and teas, liquors and wines, or serve with water to cleanse the palate between each chocolate offering.

Idea:

Buy some extra bars for table display or party favors! Give your guests a sample of each chocolate to take home and enjoy. Or, buy a large, bulk chocolate bar/piece and allow guests to "chip" off pieces during the party with a small knife or ice pick. (Keep safety in mind of course! If alcohol or small hands are around, you may not want to do this.)

Mini Parfaits

Ingredients

Crispy chocolate chip cookies (homemade are best, see page 113)

Vanilla yogurt

Fresh blueberries, raspberries, and strawberries

Whipped cream (optional)

Directions
1. Crumble the cookies.
2. Slice the strawberries (leave other berries whole).
3. In tall, clear glasses, dollop some yogurt in the bottom, then add a layer of cookie crumble, then a layer of fruit.
4. Top with some whipped cream if you like!

> Parfaits are a very simple layered dessert that may include yogurt, ice cream, or gelatin with fresh fruit and berries. Feel free to be creative! Try layering granola or crushed graham crackers instead of cookies. Parfait, in French, means "perfect," so make them perfect for your own tastes!

Mini No-Bake Cheesecakes

Ingredients

¾ cup graham cracker crumbs

3 tablespoons packed brown sugar

¼ teaspoon ground cinnamon

3 tablespoons butter, melted

1 (8-ounce) package cream cheese

1 teaspoon lemon juice

½ pint heavy whipping cream

3 tablespoons white sugar

Fresh berries for topping

Directions

1. In a small bowl, stir together the graham cracker crumbs, brown sugar, and cinnamon.
2. Add melted butter and mix well.
3. Press into the bottom of four 4-ounce ramekins.
4. Put ramekins in refrigerator to chill until firm.
5. In a medium bowl, beat together the cream cheese and lemon juice until soft.
6. Add whipping cream and beat with an electric mixer until batter thickens.
7. Add the sugar and continue to beat until stiff.
8. Pour into chilled crust.
9. Top with berries.
10. Chill several hours before serving.

Cake Pops

Ingredients

1 cup white sugar

½ cup butter

2 eggs

2 teaspoons vanilla extract

1 ½ cups all-purpose flour

1 ¾ teaspoons baking powder

½ cup milk

Directions

1. Preheat oven to 350 degrees.
2. In a medium bowl, cream together the sugar and butter. Beat in the eggs, one at a time, then stir in the vanilla.
3. Combine flour and baking powder, add to the creamed mixture, and mix well. Finally stir in the milk until batter is smooth.
4. Place liners in the cups of a mini cupcake pan, or grease and flour all the cups.
5. Pour or spoon batter into the pan, filling each cup to ⅔ full.
6. Bake 8 to 10 minutes. Mini cupcakes will be done when a tooth-pick is inserted and comes out clean.

BUTTERCREAM FROSTING

Ingredients

1 cup unsalted butter, very soft

8 cups confectioners' sugar

½ cup milk

2 teaspoons vanilla

Directions

1. Place the butter in a large mixing bowl.
2. Add 4 cups of the sugar and then the milk and vanilla.
3. Beat until smooth and creamy.
4. Gradually add the remaining sugar, 1 cup at a time, until icing is thick enough to spread easily (it's possible you may not need all of the sugar).
5. If desired, add a few drops of food coloring and mix thoroughly.

Assembly

1. Insert a popsicle into each mini cake.
2. Coat with icing.
3. If desired, coat with sprinkles, mini chocolate chips, coconut, or other items.

> For a variation, add orange or lemon extract instead of vanilla extract.

Strawberry Shortcake Sliders

MAKES APPROXIMATELY 36 MINI STRAWBERRY SHORTCAKE SLIDERS

Shortcakes

2 cups all purpose flour

2 tablespoons granulated sugar

1 tablespoon baking powder*

½ teaspoon salt

½ cup (1 stick) cold, unsalted butter (if using salted, skip the salt in dry ingredients), cut into small cubes and chilled in freezer for 15 minutes or longer

⅞ cup (that's one cup minus 2 table-spoons) heavy whipping cream

1 large egg

1 teaspoon vanilla extract

2 pints fresh strawberries, rinsed, stems removed and discarded, and sliced

¼ cup granulated sugar

Whipped Cream

1 cup heavy whipping cream

1 tablespoon granulated sugar

½ teaspoon vanilla

Directions

1. In a large bowl, vigorously whisk together the flour, sugar, salt, and baking powder.
2. Cut the butter into small cubes and add to the flour mixture and mix until the largest pieces of butter are the size of peas.
3. In a bowl, whisk together the cream, egg, and vanilla.
4. Make a well in the flour mixture and pour the cream mixture into the center of it.
5. Use a fork to stir until the dough is evenly mixed.
6. Knead the dough with your hands eight turns or so to create a ball.

7. Lightly flour a cutting board and roll the dough out until it is between ¼ and ½-inch thick. Use a small (1 ½-inch diameter or so) biscuit cutter to cut out round biscuit shapes from the dough. Place rounds on a baking sheet, spaced about 1 ½ to 2 inches apart from each other. Chill for 10 minutes in the refrigerator before baking.

8. Heat oven to 425 degrees. Bake biscuits on middle rack for 12 minutes, or until risen and lightly browned. Remove from oven and let cool.

9. To prepare the strawberries, place in a bowl and sprinkle sugar over them. Gently mix so that the sugar coats most of the strawberries. Let sit until the sugar dissolves and the strawberries release their moisture.

10. Use a hand mixer to whip the cream until it just begins to firm up. Sprinkle the sugar and vanilla over the cream. Continue to whip until it is thick and holds its shape. Cover with plastic wrap and keep chilled until it's time to assemble the mini strawberry shortcakes.

Assembly

1. When the biscuits have cooled to room temperature, gently break them apart, separating the tops from the bottoms.

2. Place several strawberry slices on each bottom, and place a dollop of whipped cream on top of the strawberries.

3. Place the top biscuit piece on top of the whipped cream.

Frozen Lime Cups

2 cups water	Zest of 2 limes
1 cup lime juice	⅔ cup sugar

1. Heat water and sugar to boiling.
2. Simmer for 5 additional minutes.
3. Remove from heat and stir in lime juice and zest.
4. Cool to room temperature.
5. Freeze until firm.
6. Shave ice into small cups.
7. Garnish with a small thin slice of lime or a few fresh berries.

JUICE CUBES

Simple as it can be! Take your favorite juice or juices, pour into ice cube trays, and freeze! Cubes can be added to drinks or placed with fruit to help keep it chilled. If you wish, you can place small slices of fruit into the trays first and then the juice.

Berry Turnovers

Pastry

½ cup granulated sugar

½ cup (1 stick) unsalted butter

2 large eggs

1 teaspoon vanilla

2 ½ cups unbleached all-purpose flour

2 teaspoons baking powder

½ teaspoon salt

Filling

4 cups fresh berries (blackberries, raspberries, blueberries, strawberries)

2 tablespoons melted butter

1 teaspoon cinnamon

1 teaspoon sugar (combined with cinnamon)

1 tablespoon flour for thickening

¼ teaspoon lemon juice

Directions

1. To make the pastry, cream the sugar and butter; beat the eggs well into the mixture until light.

2. Add the vanilla.

3. Blend together the all-purpose flour, baking powder, and salt; add to the butter mixture.

4. Blend until smooth. Chill.

5. To make the filling, combine the filling ingredients and mix well with a large spoon.

6. Preheat oven to 400 degrees. When the dough is stiff enough to be handled, turn out onto a floured board. Roll the dough out until it's about ¼-inch in thickness. Cut it into eighteen 4-inch squares. Place a heaping tablespoon of the filling in the center of the dough.

7. Fold the dough over the filling and pinch the edges together firmly. Prick the top with a fork. Dust lightly with cinnamon sugar.

8. Place on a lightly greased cookie sheet and bake on middle rack for about 15 minutes or until golden. Remove from the oven and let cool for 15 to 20 minutes (the filling will be hot at first!).

Mini Chipwiches

Ingredients

10 Mini Cookies (see page 113)
Ice cream

Directions

1. Scoop ice cream onto 5 of the cookies.
2. Place other cookie on top to form a sandwich.

Variations

Use any cookie and ice cream combination you desire!

Easy Mini Chocolate Chip Cookies

Ingredients

1 cup butter, softened

1 cup white sugar

1 cup brown sugar, packed

2 eggs

2 teaspoons vanilla extract

3 cups all-purpose flour

1 teaspoon baking soda

2 teaspoons hot water

½ teaspoon salt

2 cups semisweet chocolate chips

1 cup walnuts, chopped (optional)

Directions

1. Preheat oven to 350 degrees.
2. Cream together the butter, white sugar, and brown sugar until smooth.
3. Beat in the eggs one at a time, then stir in the vanilla.
4. Dissolve baking soda in hot water.
5. Add to cookie dough along with salt.
6. Stir in flour, chocolate chips, and walnuts, if desired.
7. Drop small spoonfuls onto ungreased pans.
8. Bake for about 10 minutes in the preheated oven, or until edges are nicely browned.

{ Libations }

Ginger Ale

Ingredients

½ cup granulated sugar

2 tablespoons grated ginger

½ lemon, juiced

1 liter plain seltzer

Directions

1. Boil 1 cup water.
2. Add sugar, grated ginger, lemon juice, and lemon rind. Bring to a boil for 3 to 4 minutes, turn down heat, and let simmer an additional 10 minutes.
3. Turn off heat and allow to cool.
4. Strain through a colander lined with a cheesecloth. Press lightly to get all liquid through but not so hard that any solid matter (lemon rind, grated ginger, etc.) gets pushed through.
5. Chill the mixture and the seltzer. (Warm seltzer fizzes easier. We want minimal fizz!)

Continued on page 118.

Variations: Carbonate with yeast. To do this, instead of using 1 liter minus 1 cup of seltzer water, use 1 liter minus 1 cup fresh water in recipe. Complete rest of recipe as written. After mix has cooled to room temperature, add ⅛ teaspoon of active baker's yeast. Place cap on container tightly. Shake to mix thoroughly. Place in warm location 24 to 48 hours. Once bottle feels hard to forcefully squeeze, place in refrigerator. Chill at least 12 hours before opening. When first opening, crack top slowly to allow excess pressure to release.

6. Once liquid and seltzer are chilled, pour out 1 cup of seltzer. Leave the rest of the seltzer in the bottle. Pour liquid mixture slowly into the seltzer bottle. Replace cap tightly. Slowly rotate bottle to mix liquid. Do not shake.

7. Chill and enjoy!

Creative drink bucket!

Get a flat-bottomed plastic container or bucket that's large enough for wine or beer bottles to sit in without touching each other and at least four inches deep. Set several empty wine or beer bottles in, fill the container with water, set in freezer, and let freeze. Ten minutes prior to guests arriving, remove the bucket from the freezer and set out to allow the ice to melt just enough that you can remove the empty bottles. Once you remove empties, place chilled white wine or beer bottles into holes. You now have a bottle holder that will keep the drinks chilled through your whole party!

Pineapple Rum Cocktails

Ingredients

1 can (46 ounces) pineapple juice
1 ¼ cups spiced rum
¾ cup coconut rum

½ cup fresh lime juice (from 6 to 8 limes)
Lime slices or pineapple slices for garnish

Directions

1. In a large pitcher, stir together pineapple juice, spiced rum, and lime juice.
2. Refrigerate 1 hour or until chilled.
3. Serve over ice, garnished with lime or pineapple slices.

Mint Lemonade

Ingredients

2 cups sugar

6 cups water

2 cups freshly squeezed lemon juice

½ cup fresh whole mint leaves

Directions

1. Combine lemon juice and water in a pitcher.
2. Slowly stir in sugar until it fully dissolves.
3. As you add, taste the lemonade for desired sweetness.
4. Once desired sweetness is achieved, stir in mint leaves.
5. Refrigerate 1 hour.
6. Serve over ice.

Alternate sweeteners

If you wish, try mixing in maple syrup, agave, honey, or another favorite sweetener. Keep in mind that some sweeteners are stronger than others, so vary amount used accordingly.

For a sparkling version, substitute 6 cups chilled seltzer instead of water.

Punch Bowl

Ingredients

4 cups orange juice

4 cups guava juice (mango or apricot nectar can be substituted if guava juice is not available)

4 cups pineapple juice

½ cup cherry juice (not sour cherry)

4 ½ cups ginger ale

Directions

Mix all ingredients in a large punch bowl and stir gently. Add ice, sherbet, or prefreeze some juice cubes to add just before serving!

This is a simple drink that can be made exquisite with easy variations. For instance, rather than buying ginger ale, use the homemade ginger ale on page 116! Add fresh citrus or seasonal fruit slices as garnish, some mint leaves, or, for a grown-up version, add a few splashes of rum.

Hot Chocolate

MAKES 4 SERVINGS

Ingredients

4 tablespoons cocoa powder

8 tablespoons sugar

8 tablespoons water

4 cups milk

Directions

Combine cocoa, sugar, and water in a small saucepan. Heat over low heat, stirring to prevent the ingredients from sticking to the pan. After a minute, add milk. Continue stirring until heated.

> Add a bit of vanilla, mint, or orange extract for a different flavor. Serve with homemade marshmallows (page 90).

Citrus Fizz

Ingredients

1 liter orange seltzer

½ cup fresh lemon juice

½ cup sugar

3 ounces vodka (optional)

Ice cubes

Directions

1. Combine seltzer, lemonade, lemon juice, and vodka, if using.

2. Pour over ice.

3. Garnish with lemon or orange slices.

Raspberry Spritzer

Ingredients

2 cups plain seltzer

⅔ cup frozen raspberries

2 sprigs fresh mint

3 ounces Chambord

Ice cubes

Directions

1. Combine seltzer, raspberries, mint, and Chambord.
2. Pour over ice.

Iced Tea

Ingredients

5 tea bags (black, green, or white)   ¾ cup lemon juice

5 cups water   ½ cup honey

Ice (about 2 cups)

Directions

1. Boil 5 cups of water.
2. Turn off heat and put tea bags in the water.
3. Let steep 2 to 3 minutes, stirring occasionally.
4. Remove tea bags and squeeze to drain out any extra liquid. Add honey and stir well.
5. Add 2 cups of ice into the tea and put in the fridge to chill for 4 to 5 minutes (not so long that the ice melts).
6. Take out of fridge and stir in the lemon juice.

> Try making with a fruity tea or using maple syrup as your sweetener.

Strawberry Banana Pineapple Smoothies

MAKES 6 SERVINGS

Ingredients

½ pint fresh strawberries, stems removed

½ fresh pineapple, peeled, cored, and chopped

2 ripe bananas, peeled

¾ cup water

2 cups medium ice cubes

Directions

1. Combine ingredients.
2. Process in blender until smooth.
3. Serve immediately or freeze until slushy.

Variations:

Sweeten a little with honey, maple syrup, or your other favorite sweetener (about 3 tablespoons).

Try using coconut water rather than regular water.

Add a little rum or other alcohol if desired.

Creamsicle Drink

Ingredients

2 cups orange juice

1 cup milk

1 cup water

½ cup powdered sugar

1 teaspoon vanilla extract

9 whole ice cubes

Directions

Combine all ingredients in blender and blend until smooth.

Index